WHAT LIVES IN A LAMP AND SOLVES MATHS PROBLEMS?

A GENIE-US!

COURT JESTERS

ALL RISE! BE UPSTANDING!

EH?

ALL RISE!

WHAT'S GOING ON

Then —

BEANOTOWN COURT

PONK! SWISH!

LET'S SEE TEACHER IN ACTION.

GREAT! I LOVE TENNIS!

Wrong sort of court, Smiffy.

In court.

BRING IN THE PERSON ACCUSED OF BAG SNATCHING!

YES, M'LUD!

GROWL!

OO . . . ER!

WE'LL SEE HOW A TRIAL IN COURT WORKS!

ZZZZ! SNORE! SNORT!

OKAY, GENTLY DOES IT! I'M GOING TO TAKE HIS PLACE!

BANG! BANG!

ERK!

WAH!

FLIP!

CALL — HEADS OR TAILS!

ZZZZZZ

EH? ER . . . TAILS!

HEADS! HARD LUCK — GO TO JAIL FOR 10,000 YEARS!

CATCH

GASP!

THE HEEL'S FALLEN OFF MY SHOE. WHAT CAN I DO?

YOU COULD ALWAYS TRY LIMPING!

PUT IT TO YOU THAT SHALL NOT BE HERE THE REST OF THE DAY! STATE MY CASE THAT M NEEDED IN COURT!

I'M ON JURY DUTY! WINSTON'S IN CHARGE!

SPARE MORTAR BOARD

PURR!

HO-HO!

I'LL GET OUR NEW 'TEACHER' TO AGREE TO THIS!

POUR

MILK

TAKE THE REST OF THE DAY OFF —

SIGNED -

MEOW! YUM! SLURP!

GOOD OLD WINSTON!

PLONK

FISH FINGERS

ALL THE EYE TNESS TO THE THEFT!

AHA! HE DID IT! I'M SURE! HIM! YES . . . HIM!

EH?

GASP! THIS IS GOING TO TAKE ALL DAY!

HAR-HAR!

Much later —

I THEN NOTICED THE ACCUSED . . .

ZZZZ!

ZZZZ!

ZZZ!

SUGAR DUMMY

I KNOW HOW TO SPEED THINGS UP! A NEW JUDGE IS NEEDED!

ZZZZ! SNORT! ZZZZ!

TIPTOE

WAIT A MINUTE, YOUR ONOUR! I MUST PROTEST! YOU CAN'T JUST TOSS A COIN — WHAT ABOUT THE JURY? I WANT TO HAVE MY SAY! I DEMAND TO BE GIVEN TIME . . .

HMM!

YOU'LL BE GIVEN 'TIME' OKAY — 10,000 YEARS IN JAIL FOR CHEEK! TAKE HIM AWAY!

SWISH

WOW!

I ALSO RECOMMEND THAT EVERYONE IN COURT SHALL BE GIVEN FREE ICE-CREAM AND POP-CORN FOR THE REST OF THE DAY!

SLURP! ANOTHER TRIUMPH FOR BRITISH JUSTICE! SLOO!

SLURP! YAHOO!

PUSH

CHOMP!

ICE CREAM

POP CORN

POP CORN

POP CORN

SWISH

THE HEADMASTER WOULD LIKE A WORD WITH YOU BEFORE WE GO TO TAKE PART IN THE BEANOTOWN INTER-SPORTS DAY!

PLEASE, PLEASE BRING BACK A TROPHY FOR OUR DISPLAY CABINET THIS YEAR! PLEASE!

BUT WE DO BRING BACK SOMETHING EACH YEAR, YOUR HEADSHIP!

PLEAD

WE BRING A WOODEN SPOON BACK EVERY YEAR!

HUMPH!

SPIN

WHEEE

HOI!

WHUMP

RUIN MY CHANCES OF A PRIZE, EH?

SIGH! THEY THOUGHT THE SAND WAS FOR A SANDCASTLE COMPETITION!

BIFF HIM!

BOOT

WHUMP

Next.

ARE YOU SURE YOU CAN THROW IT, 'ERBERT?

YES, SIR! I CAN THROW IT FOR MILES!

SPIN

EH? BUT?

ZOOM

ZOOM

THAT'S IT, FATTY! FASTER!

ZOOM

WE'VE WON A TROPHY!

YAHOO!

WINNING POST

ZOOM

DING

...AY CABINET

BURST OPEN

AAGH!

...HA! A SPOON ...R BEING LAST!

AHEM! LET'S GO, CLASS!

CHORTLE!

At the Sports Ground.

PHEW! IS IT GRUB TIME YET?

AHEM! DO YOUR BEST, KIDS!

YAWN!

RUMBLE

TRAMP THUD

WE'RE SURE TO WIN A PRIZE IN THIS EVENT!

WE'VE TRAINED ALL SUMMER!

...! OFF IN THE ...G DIRECTION!

EH?

...HROW

BELL

HOI! MY HAT!

ZIP

IT'S THE FINAL RACE! WE'LL WIN THIS ONE, SIR!

SIGH! I DON'T THINK SO!

Soon —

FATTY'S GOING TO RUN IT FOR US!

EH? ME!

PUSH

G...GASP!

BANG!

ZOOM

ZOOM

ZOOM

GO, FATTY! GO!

...T HOW DID YOU GET FATTY TO RUN LIKE THAT?

EASY! WE TIED HIS PACKED LUNCH ONTO THE BACKS OF THE OTHER RUNNERS!

ONCE HE WAS MOVING AT SPEED, FATTY'S WEIGHT CARRIED HIM ON! HA-HA!

Later, back at school.

IT'S SUPER THAT WE'VE WON A TROPHY . . . BUT IT'S JUST AS WELL WE HAD WON SO MANY WOODEN SPOONS BEFORE!

YUM! BECAUSE THE HEAD'S FILLED THE CUP WITH ICE CREAM TO CELEBRATE!

SLURP!

SUCK! SLURP!

SLOO!

SLOO!

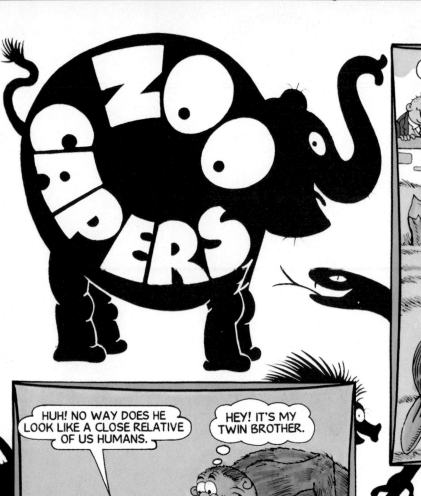

WHAT DID THE JUDGE SAY TO THE SKUNK?

ODOUR IN COURT.

DOES IT!

HUH! I SUPPOSE WE HAVE TO GO TO SCHOOL!

BASH ST. SCHOOL —

GASP!

NO WE DON'T!

IT'S GONE!

Then —

HA-HA! THIS WAY, KIDS!

EH? WHAT'S GOING ON?

GASP! BUT THAT'S FAKE FOOD, MADE FROM PLASTER AND WOOD!

GOBBLE! CHOMP! VERY NICE! CHOMP!

HO-HO! IT'S STILL BETTER THAN SCHOOL DINNERS!

SIGH! VERY TRUE!

HUH! STAND BACK, GIRLIE! WE'RE TOUGH STUNT MEN!

TUMBLE

THUMP

TUM... TEE... TUM!

BIFF

YEAH! YOU MIGHT GET HURT! HAW-HAW!

SNARL! WIMPS!

GLAD YOU LIKE THE LOOK OF MY SOUP, MISTER SPIELSNACK. AN EXTRA HELPING FOR YOU AT LUNCHTIME! CHORTLE!

HA-HA! LOOK — MISTER SPIELSNACK'S A MONSTER. A BIG GREEN ONE! ·

WELL, TEACHER. I WANT TO FILM RAGE... ANGER...

OKAY!

TITTER!

OO... YOU NAUGHTY CHILDREN! AHEM... BAD PUPILS...

CUT! CUT! NO USE.

HE'S TOO SOFT!

I WAS BEHIND THIS SCREEN. THIS IS A TRICK USED BY THE FILM CREW MAKING A PICTURE HERE TODAY!

FILM CREW?

SLURP!

YES! STEVEN SPIELSNACK'S HERE TO USE THE SCHOOL IN A BLOCKBUSTER FILM!

WOW!

YUM! DROOL!

STOP, FATTY!

BIFF!

HUH! SOFTIES!

ER . . . PERHAPS YOU COULD HELP?

THE FILM'S A KUNG FU, COWBOY, MYSTERY COWBOY FILM. WE NEED A SWAMP!

NO PROBLEM, STEVEN!

So —

PERFECT! JUST PERFECT!

SWAMPY PONG!

SIGH! NO USE!

WE COULD HELP!

HEH-HEH! PERFECT! AN EASY WAY WE KNOW TO MAKE TEACHER ANGRY!

SNARL! GRRRR!

SNARL! GRRR . . . AN AWFUL MESS . . . SNORT!

. . . HAND IN OUR HOMEWORK JOTTERS! HO-HO-HO!

EEK!

WHIRR

DIRECTOR

WAA!

PUP PARADE

WHAT HAS ONE FOOT IN YOUR DESSERT?

STORK-INFESTED CUSTARD.

INTO CLASS AT ONCE! THIS WAY . . . NOW!

SPLAT

DING DONG

PUFF

FLUMP

. . . FATTY . . . TOOTS . . . DANNY . . .

TUG

TUG

. . . NEW BOY . . . SMIFFY . . .

LET'S GO BEFORE TEACHER RECOVERS!

YIPPEE! OUT TO PLAY IN THE SNOW!

ZOOM

SLAM SHUT

SPLAT

NOT SO FAST! YOU'RE STAYING INDOORS, KIDS!

THROW

AW!

WHEEEE

Soon —

ART LESSON N

HUMP

PLOP

YOU TELL ME, SIR. HAVE A LOOK!

HMM . . . YES . . . A FISH? BOAT . . .?

SPIN

PUSH

SPIN

PUSH

OOOOOOOOH!

HO-HO! TEACHER'S HYPNOTISED! I'D SEEN THIS DONE ON THE TV ONCE!

CHORTLE!

SPIN

WHAT IS A LUMBERJACK'S FAVOURITE NURSERY RHYME?

CHAINSAW MARJORY DAW!

DANGER

WAIT! A NEW PUPIL! OUT HERE AT ONCE, BOY!

HE'LL BE OUT IN A MINUTE, SIR!

2 + 1 =
2 + 2 =
2 + 3 =
2 + 4 =
2 + 5 =

HERE HE COMES, SIR!

WOW! ER . . .

2 + 5 =

YEAAGH!

HAR-HAR!

SWOOSH

SPLAT

WHAT ARE YOU PAINTING, SMIFFY?

DAB!

A PICTURE CALLED — 'A VIEW FROM THE WINDOW'!

EEAGH!

PITY IT'S SNOWING!

HMM! AN ABSTRACT! WHAT DOES IT MEAN, DANNY?

YOU WILL OBEY ME, TEACHER. WE SHALL ALL GO OUTSIDE AND PLAY IN THE SNOW!

WOW! IT WORKED!

WE SHALL! WHO'D LIKE A SNOWBALL FIGHT?

HMM! VERY ODD! WHAT IS TEACHER TEACHING THEM OUT THERE?

THROW

SPLAT

SPLAT

SPLAT

CHORTLE! HE COULDN'T TEACH US ANYTHING — ABOUT HOW TO GET OUT OF DOING BORING WORK!

WHEN DID NAPOLEON NOTICE HE HAD A BUNION?

WHEN HE WAS STARING DE-FEET IN THE FACE.

OH . . . YES, MRS TEACHER! TEACHER'S ILL, EH? HE'LL NOT MANAGE IN TO SCHOOL TODAY! ER . . . OKAY!

WAHEY!

NO TEACHER!

THAT'S WHERE YOU LOT ARE WRONG! I HAVE A LONG LIST OF TEACHERS I CAN CALL OUT IF SOMEONE'S ILL!

OH!

BOO!

LIST OF SUPPLY TEACHERS

UNROLL

NOT SO FAST! I HAVE A SUPPLY TEACHER HERE TO LOOK AFTER YOU!

BUMP

ZONK

TA-RA! YOUR TEACHER FOR THE DAY!

GASP! SMIFFY'S MUM!

HM—

SUPPLIES! SUPPLIES!

But—

1. IF ONE FISH COSTS THREE APPLES AND TWO DOGS EAT ONE WHALE — HOW MANY PEOPLE ARE STUCK IN THE LIFT AT THE FOURTH FLOOR?

2. TAKE ONE CUP OF SUGAR, ADD AN EGG, HEAT WELL THEN TAKE IT AWAY FROM A HANDFUL OF APES — HOW MANY CATS ARE LEFT?

3. ONE PLUS A FISH FINGER TAKE AWAY A SEVEN EQUALS?

WE CAN'T GO TILL WE'VE DONE THESE IMPOSSIBLE PROBLEMS!

EH?

WHAT?

AHEM!

AHA . . . YES! I KNOW THE ANSWERS TO THAT . . . AND THAT . . .

SNAP!

GOOD, GIRL! WELL DONE! ALL CORRECT!

PHEW! SMIFFY'S THE ONLY ONE IN CLASS ABLE TO FILL IN ANY ANSWERS!

MUMBLE! MUMBLE!

Smiffy
1 Sausage ✓
2 fish ✓
3 Balloons

TICK

CUTHBERT

WHAT DO YOU CALL A CHEF WHO TALKS RUBBISH?

GOBBLEDECOOK.

AHEM! SO YOU'RE SUDDENLY OFF TO OUTER MONGOLIA, EH?

EH-HEH!

SIGH! ONLY ONE NAME LEFT TO TRY! THEY ALL SEEM TO BE OKAY UNTIL I MENTION THAT IT'S CLASS IIB!

HO-HO! LET'S GO AND PLAY IN CLASS!

NO TEACHER WANTS TO COME AND TEACH US!

Soon, in class.

NNNNGH!

LET'S GO AND SAIL OUR BOATS ON BASH STREET POND!

SAW

PENCILS

OD CHRISTMAS!

DON'T I KNOW YOU?

ER . . . I WAS JUST THINKING THAT MYSELF, SIR!

SCRATCH!

SCRATCH!

WHAT DO YOU DO TODAY?

WE USUALLY GET TO TAKE OUR BOATS OUT TO SAIL ON THE POND, MRS SMIFFY!

CLASS IIB

SOUNDS OKAY — BUT WE'LL HAVE A LITTLE TEST FIRST!

HA-HA! IT'LL BE SIMPLE SUMS!

EVEN WE'LL BE ABLE TO SOLVE THEM!

WINK

WE'LL NOT GET OUT TO SAIL OUR BOATS — BUT NO MATTER!

WAAAA! SOB! BLUB! BEATEN IN A TEST BY SMIFFY! WAAA!

SPLOOSH

WAHEY!

HO-HO! CUTHBERT, THE CLASS SWOT, IS SO UPSET AT BEING BEATEN IN THE 'TEST' BY SMIFFY — HE'S CREATING ANOTHER BASH STREET POND!

GREAT FUN!

PUSH

BE A SPORT

FLOWERY LANGUAGE

WHERE'S TEACHER?

OO...SUPER PLANTS! NICE TO MEET YOU!

EH?

WHAT A HANDSOME PLANT YOU ARE!

HA-HA! TEACHER'S GONE BONKERS!

KISS!

HE'S TALKING TO PLANTS!

NOPE! LOOK! HI, SMIFFY! NICE DAY! HOW ARE YOU?

NICE FISH...BLEEP! I'LL HAVE SIX PENCE WORTH! NO...I'M A WEEK LATE... BLOOP!

OH, YES! A LOST CAUSE!

FATTY TALKS TO A PIE NOW AND AGAIN!

SLURP! SLURP!

OO...NICE LOOKING PIE! YUM!

MUNCH! CHOMP!

FATTY DOESN'T CHAT LONG THOUGH!

SIR! SOME VERY LONELY TREES OVER HERE!

SHAME! I'LL COME OVER AND CHAT TO THEM!

HELLO, MISTER TREE. YOU DO LOOK NICE!

SHALL I GIVE YOU A HUG IT'LL MAKE YOU FEEL BETT

S NOT A DAFT IDEA
ALK TO PLANTS — IT
PS THEM TO GROW!

HO-HO! I'LL TRY IT!

HELLO, PLANT! HOW'S IT GOING?

But —

GASP! IT'S TOO CRUEL FOR YOU TO STARE AT A PLANT, PLUG!

HUMPH!

WILT

DROOP

MIND YOU, WE TALK TO A THICK PIECE OF WOOD EVERY DAY!

OH, REALLY. DOES IT RESPOND TO YOU?

SNIFF

BUT THE PIE OFTEN TALKS BACK!

BLOOP!

Then —

LET'S GO OUT TO THE PARK AND TALK TO MORE PLANTS!

HELLO . . . HELLO! NICE TO SEE YOU!

HMM! I WONDER!

O — YOU CAN EAR OFF, MATE!

DOH!

WHAP!

TEE-HEE!

TUG!

ARMY CAMOUFLAGE TRAINING GROUND

OOOH!

CHEEK!

THROB

CHORTLE! THAT 'TREE' DIDN'T LIKE BEING TALKED TO AT ALL, SIR!

LET'S HAVE A GAME OF FOOTBALL! TEACHER'S TALKING TO HIMSELF NOW!

LEFT . . . RIGHT . . . LEFT . . .

ACHE!
PAIN!
THROB!

OOH! YOU SILLY OLD FOOL! WHY DON'T YOU GIVE UP TALKING TO PLANTS AND VERY RUDE TREES?

WHO WAS NOAH'S WIFE?

JOAN OF ARK!

WE HATE SCHOOL!

TOO MANY RULES!

YEAH!

DON'T STAND THERE! RULE 11A!

DON'T WALK ON THAT SIDE OF THE CORRIDOR! RULE 183B!

BROOM CUPBOARD

WHAT'S GOING ON HERE?

GASP! A PRISON RIOT! ALL BECAUSE OF TOO MANY RULES!

THUMP! BANG!

BIFF! THUD!

BEANO TOWN JAIL

AHA! LET'S HAVE A WORD WITH THE PRISONERS TO SEE IF A RIOT WORKS!

YOO-HOO!

BEANO TOWN JAIL

GOOD OL' SM

WHIMPER!

KEEP AWAY!

SLAMSHUT

CLICK CLOSED

SLAMSHUT

BUT . . . WE ONLY WANT A CHAT WITH YOU!

WOW! A BIT TOUGH ON THE POOR PRISONERS — SENDING IN THE BASH STREET KIDS AS A RESCUE PARTY — BUT . . . NO HARM DONE!

BUT WE DIDN'T GET A CHANCE TO CHAT TO ANY PRISONERS ABOUT RULES!

Prison Governor.

HUM

CLICK OPEN

P R I S O N

R I O T

HMM! THIS IS JUST ABOUT THE ONLY THING YOU CAN DO WITHOUT BREAKING A SCHOOL RULE!

WE'LL SEE!

HMMM!

K PIE

LIST OF RULES

HOP BACKWARD

HOP!

In the playground.

SIGH! IT'S LIKE BEING IN PRISON!

TALKING OF WHICH — WHAT'S GOING ON OVER AT BEANOTOWN PRISON?

THROW

BEANOTOWN PRISON

MAIN GATE

WA-OO WA-OO WA-OO WA-OO

SCREECH SCREECH

SNARL! WHO DARES TO DISTURB US DURING OUR RIOT?

GRUNT! YEAH! NO MANNERS!

CRACK!

SMASH!

CRACK

WHEE!

THUD!

HOI! LET US IN! WE WANT A WORD!

EEK! THE BASH STREET KIDS!

WAA! RUN FOR IT, CEDRIC!

HOI! WAIT!

ZOOM

PRISON RIOT OVER! I'M RESCUED THANKS TO THE KIDS!

SMILE PLEASE!

CLICK

Shortly —

THANK YOU, KIDS! HERE'S A HAMPER OF GRUB MADE UP IN OUR OWN PRISON KITCHEN!

SLURP!

COO!

Back in class.

CHOMP!

PILE-CAKE

SAUSAGE BARS

TUCK!

HELP!

CHEW

JELLY

YAHOO!

SPLURGE

JELLY

CLANG

IRON

WAH!

CHEW

CHOMP! SAUSAGE BARS!

DON'T WORRY, READERS. IT ISN'T A RIOT— ONLY THE KIDS HAVING A PARTY! SIGH! A RIOT MIGHT HAVE BEEN LESS CHAOTIC!

WHERE DID MOBILE PHONES ORIGINATE?

CALIPHONEYA.

BOOK IN FOR LAUGHS

In class.

OKAY, READING TIME. GET YOUR BOOKS OUT!

OPEN

WAH! WHAT'S THAT YOU'RE READING?

PING PING PING SPLUTTER SPLUT

RICE CRISPIE

THE BACK OF A CEREAL BOX, SIR!

Shortly.

TISK! AS I SUSPECTED — THIS LIBRARY HASN'T BEEN TOUCHED IN YEARS!

SCHOOL LIBRARY

Inside.

HMM! ONLY A FEW ANCIENT BOOKS HERE!

MMM! I'M SURE WE HAD MORE BOOKS THAN THIS!

MODERN ENGLISH MATHS HISTOR

HUH!

MAYBE THE BEANO ARTIST CAN HELP ME TO GET THOSE DREADFUL PUPILS TO READ GOOD BOOKS!

TUM . . . TEE . . . TUM!

HAPPY AT HIS WORK

PAINT BOX DOOR

Later.

YOU ARE NOW GOING TO STUDY THE FINEST WORKS OF ENGLISH LITERATURE!

SCHOOL LIBRARY

GROAN!

BOO!

TERRIFIC!

BRILLIAN

THIS IS GREAT!

HUH! NO GOOD. THE WRITING'S TOO SMALL FOR ME TO READ!

ONCE UPON A TIME

THERE WAS A LITTLE BOY.

AT LEAST SMIFFY BROUGHT A DECENT BOOK!

FLIP FLIP

IT'S A GOOD BOOK — BUT THE LIST OF CHARACTERS IS A BIT LONG!

SLAM SHUT

PHONE BOOK

PLOOP!

WHAT'S THE MATTER WITH YOU LOT? DOESN'T ANYONE USE THE SCHOOL LIBRARY?

LIB-LUB-LY?

TUG

DID HE SAY 'LAVATORY'?

WE LEFT SOME OUTSIDE THE FOOTBALL GROUND!

I TOOK SOME HOME TO REPLACE THE CHAIRS I KEPT BREAKING!

I USED SOME FOR PAPER MACHE!

WATER

WHAT A HANDSOME MODEL I MADE!

WOW! TEACHER HAD THE BEANO ARTIST DRAW COMIC STRIP VERSIONS OF FAMOUS BOOKS!

THIS IS A GREAT STORY!

TREASURE ISLAND

WUTHERING HEIGHTS
HEATHCLIFFE!

MACBETH
BEGONE, WITCHES!

OLIVER TWIST
MORE PLEASE!
NO!
SPLUDGE

HAR-HAR!

OLIVER

LIFT!

WE'RE NOT EATING THAT!

FLING!

TOSS!

HURL!

GOOD RIDDANCE!

Outside, something stirs —

MUNCH!

CHOMP!

SCHOOL LAWN

OO-ER! SOUND LIKE SOMETHIN' EATING OLIVE PIE.

SURELY NO—

HMPH! YOU CAN JOLL WELL GO BACK TO YOUR CLASS HUNGRY THEN!

BYOING!

NOT TO MENTION THIS FROG!

IT'S LUCKY WE DIDN'T EAT IT!

Meanwhile —

SIR! SIR! YOU WANTED US TO BRING A SPECIMEN OF NATURE. WELL, I'VE BROUGHT ONE, SIR.

SPLENDID, CUTHBERT, MY NUMBER-ONE SWOT.

UGH! A HORRIBLE LITTLE SLUG — AND IT REMINDS ME OF YOU, CUTHBERT!

GET UP, BOY, AND UNHAND MY TROUSERS.

GROVEL!

SOB! YOU DON'T M— I'M A CRAWLER DO YOU, SIR?

A BIG, SHINY APPLE, SIR.

BUT YOU ALWAYS BRING ME AN APPLE, CUTHBERT.

SURELY NOT, SIR!

CHOMP!

THE BASH STREET KIDS
in BEASTIE PLOYS

THUD!

GOSH! THIS POOR DOG MUST BE LOST.

WE CAN'T LEAVE HIM TO STRAY.

MAP

WAG!

WAG!

YOU CAN COME TO SCHOOL WITH US, BOY.

TEACHER TREATS US LIKE DOGS ANYWAY.

SCHOOL

NO ANIMALS ON SCHOOL PREMISES – BEGONE, DOG!

BUT HE'S NOWHERE TO GO, SIR.

WHIMPER!

HOW'D YOU LIKE TO BE HOUNDED OUT?

AT PLAYTIME —

ROTTEN OLD TEACHER HATES ANIMALS ALMOST AS MUCH AS HE HATES US.

YES! BUT I'VE GOT AN IDEA.

CHOOL

WE'LL DRIVE TEACHER BATTY!

OFF HIS CHIMP EVEN!

BASH STREET ANIMAL SANCTUARY

~ ALL WELCOME

SHORTLY —

RIGHT, PONDLIFE! IT'S TIME FOR A MEGA-BORING LESSON IN HISTORY.

AHA! SOMETHING IS AFOOT.

CREAK OPEN

HISSSS!

NYERK!

HO-HO! DID YOU SAY HISS-TORY, SIR?

WOW! SOMETHING'S ABOUT TEN FOOT!

SLITHER!

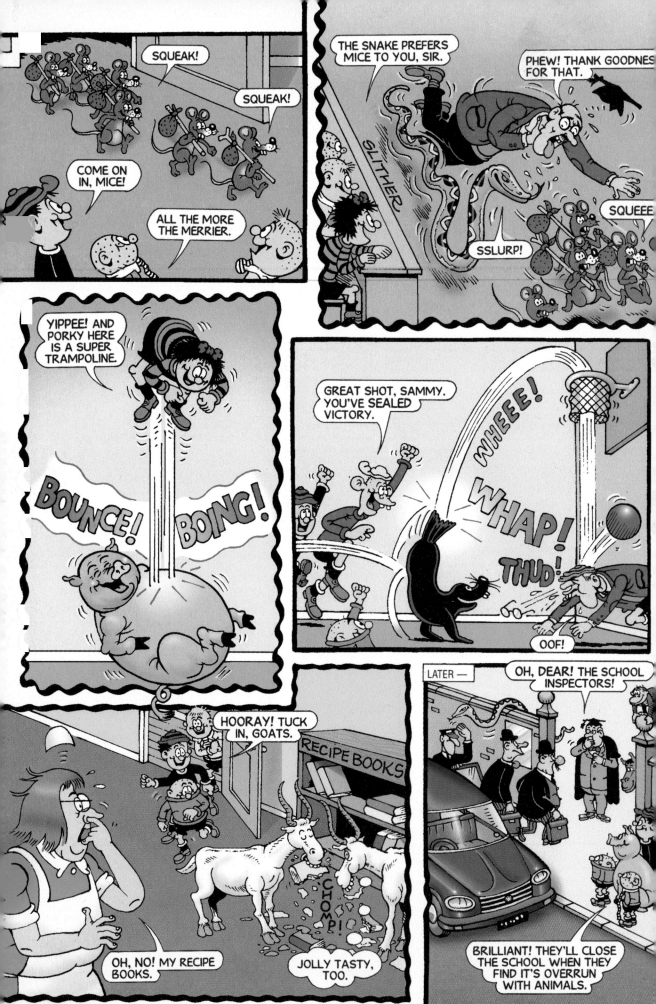

INTO YOUR P.E. CLASS, YOU LOT – AND NO MORE ANIMAL ANTICS.

OKAY!

SCHOOL GYM

LEAP!

WAHEY! SUPER VAULTING HORSE.

BOUNCE!

NEDDY THE CLYDESDALE'S COME TO STAY AS WELL.

THE SCHOOL KITCHEN —

AP!

AP!

TSK! WHO'S BADGERING ME WHEN I'M COOKING THE KIDS' LUNCHES?

CHIL PEPP

RED HOT PEPP

GARL

AAGH! NO THANKS, BADGER. I DON'T REQUIRE WORMS FOR MY SPROUT 'N' PILCHARD PIE.

S-S-S

XCELLENT IDEA, HEADMASTER.

THE SCHOOL NEEDED A DIFFERENT APPROACH.

BASH STREET ANIMAL SANCTUARY ~ALL WELCOME

PET WOOD WORM

ANIMALS WILL BE MUCH EASIER TO TEACH THAN THIS UNRULY SHOWER.

BASH ST. SCHOOL

BASH STREET ANIMAL SANCTUARY ALL WELCOME

OUT YOU GO!

HEY! BUT THIS IS OUR SCHOOL.

WE LIKE IT HERE – SORT OF!

ANTI-SOCIAL CLIMBER KIDS

INTO THE HALL. IT'S TIME FOR A P.E. LESSON!

GYM HALL

JOG

But —

OOF!

ZONK!

THUD!

DOH! WHO PUT THIS PIECE OF CLIFF HERE?

DAZED

I FIND CLIMBING VERY EASY!

MY EARS ARE GREAT FOR HANGING ON WITH! HO-HO!

GRIP

STICK

But —

SQUALK!

ER . . . NICE BIRDIE!

I WOULDN'T SAY THAT, TEACHER!

PLOOP

PLOOP

PLOOP

HEH-HEH!

THE JANITOR

HUMPH!

HO-HO!

I'M READY FOR P.E. NOW!

PLP PLP

Editor's note:— 'Silly boy'

WHAT IS YOUR FAVOURITE BUILDING, FATTY?

THE TRIFLE TOWER, SIR.

ISN'T IT GREAT? I HAD A BUILDER MAKE THIS CLIFF-FACE TO HELP YOU ALL GET INTO THE LATEST SPORT OF 'ROCK CLIMBING'!

EH? OH! SUPER, YOUR HEADSHIP!

Soon —

COO . . . EE! LOOK HOW HIGH I AM ALREADY!

HUMPH! CHEAT!

SUPER, SIR! WE'LL HAVE A GO!

WATCH OUT, CLASS!

AAARGH!

PECK

WELL DONE, SIR!

GOOD CATCH! HA-HA-HA!

BITE

CRASH!

And —

WHEEE

HUMPH! THERE'S NO CHANCE OF EVER CLIMBING THIS CLIFF!

TUG

CRACK

CRASH

OOPS!

TRIP

THANKS TO SMIFFY — IT'S MUCH EASIER TO CLIMB NOW! CHORTLE!

DAZED

HOP

GRRR!

AHEM! INTERESTED IN A ROCKERY FOR YOUR GARDEN, YOUR HEADSHIP?

HOW DID THE HIPPOPOTOMUS LOSE WEIGHT?

IT WENT FOR HIPPO-SUCTION.

JEST THE JOB

WE'RE LATE FOR SCHOOL.

KNOW ANY GOOD EXCUSES, READERS?

PUSH

IIB

ERK! TEACHER SPOTTED US

WHAT'S THE MEANING OF THIS NOISE? HOW DARE YOU?

AH, HEAD! THE VERY MAN.

DONK

I JUST WANT TO SAY ONE THING . . .

PROD

RRRRASP TO YOU, FAT STUFF!

GASP!

GIGGLE!

OUT! GET O YOU'RE SAC

ZONK

LOOKS LIKE I'LL HAVE TO TEACH THE CLASS. IT'S YEARS SINCE I GAVE LESSONS . . .

. . . SHARPEN YOUR QUILLS AND WE'LL BEGIN.

CERTAINLY HAS BEEN A LONG TIME.

After school —

SCHOOL

HUH! HEAD WAS WORSE THAN TEACHER.

BORING!

CARROTS — TWENTY PENCE A POUND! LOVELY CARROTS!

SUPER-MARKET

EH? THAT VOICE SOUN FAMILIAR.

WHY DID THE NURSE WAKE UP HER PATIENTS?

TO GIVE THEM THEIR SLEEPING PILLS.

KIDS! LATE ...N, EH? WELL, ...HO CARES?

CUPPA

WHAT A LOAD OF TRIPE. HAW-HAW-HAW!

HOME-WORK JOTTERS

1 + 1 = 6! WHAT A LAUGH!

PUZZLED

LET'S FORGET WORK AND HAVE SOME CHOCCIE BICCIES AS A TREAT.

...HO CARES? ...NOT ME ...

...I GOT A PHONE CALL OFFERING ME A JOB IN MARKETING AND PROMOTIONS. STICK YOUR JOB UP YOUR NOSE!

I'M OFF TO MY FIRST BIT OF WORK AT A LARGE SUPERMARKET IN TOWN!

SNIP

HE MUST BE GOING TO OPEN THE SUPERMARKET, COS HE'S SO FAMOUS.

BYEE FOR EVER!

AHEM! I MADE A SLIGHT MISTAKE. MY MARKETING AND PROMOTIONS JOB MEANS I'VE TO DRESS UP AS A CARROT.

Back at school —

I DO HOPE YOU DIDN'T TAKE MY LITTLE JOKE ABOUT LEAVING SERIOUSLY, YOUR GLORIOUSNESS!

HARUMPH!

YUM-YUM!

SCHOOL VEGETABLE PATCH

LOOKS LIKE TEACHER WANTS HIS JOB BACK.

I JUST MIGHT GIVE HIM HIS JOB BACK AFTER WE'VE ALL WATCHED THIS GREAT ENTERTAINMENT.

WAH! HELP!

BITE

LEAP

HAR-HAR!

TODAY'S MENU CARROT SOUP

...A PIECE OF
E IS ALWAYS
I CARRY ONE...

DAZED

...AROUND MY WAIST! OOOH!

TUG

SPIN

HA-HA! YES — VERY HANDY!

FLOP DOWN

HUMPH! YOU CHEEKY LOT!

GRRR! AS A PUNISHMENT YOU'LL ALL FIND ME TEN USES FOR ROPE!

HO-HO!

SQUEAL! WAIL!

LOOK! SID'S USING A ROPE IN HIS 'ROPE TRICK', SIR!

I MUST STOP THIS RACKET! IT'S GIVING ME A SORE HEAD!

RAM

GLOOP!

SPLAASH!

AAGH!

WHEN YOU STOP THE MUSIC — DOWN COMES THE ROPE AND BOTTLE OF RED INK!

NNNNGH!

TUG

DRIP

DRIP

WHAT ARE YOU DOING WITH THAT ROPE, SMIFFY?

HO-HO! GOOD OLD TEACHER! EVEN THOUGH HE'S IN A SPOT OF TROUBLE...

! A BULL IN THE ROOM BAD ENOUGH! BUT WE'RE GLAD WE'RE OT COVERED IN RED INK! CHORTLE!

...HE STILL HAS TIME TO DEMONSTRATE ANOTHER USE FOR A PIECE OF ROPE!

GRUNT! SNORT!

OO...NICE BULL!

THUMP OF HOOVES

HA-HA! MAKING A ROPE LADDER!

HORSING AROUND

CHOMP! MUNCH!

'BYEEE, DOBBIN!

WE'D BETTE TO SCHOOL

DOH! WHAT'S THE BIG IDEA BRINGING A HORSE TO SCHOOL!

BUT, SIR — DOBBIN JUST FOLLOWED US!

STAGGER

GASP! THE HEAD!

TEACHER! I'D LIKE A WORD WITH YOU!

WE'LL DISGUISE DOBBIN, SIR!

So —

THERE!

PLOP

BUMP

I HOPE IT WORKS!

PHEW! DOBBIN WILL HAVE TO LEAVE!

AW! BUT HE WAS GOING TO HELP US WITH OUR MATHS, SIR!

EH? MATHS . . . BUT . . . HOW?

FOUR FAULTS

TWO FAULTS

FOUR PLUS TWO EQUALS . . . ER . . . AHEM!

KICK!

LEAP

KICK!

TOPPLE!

CHORTLE! WELL, PERHAPS DOBBIN CAN BE USEFUL!

HO-HO! HE WANTS TO COME WITH US!

CHORTLE!

DRING DRING

WHERE ARE THE KIDS?

HA-HA!

ZOOM

AARGH!

SQUASH

CLIP CLOP

IIB

HAVE ANOTHER IDEA!

TEA, SIR?

OOO! GREAT!

SLOO! SLURP!

AHA! A NEW PUPIL! YES — YOU LOOK LIKE A BRIGHT SPARK! NICE TO MEET YOU!

GLASSES ALL STEAMED UP!

TITTER!

INNNNNG!

THUD! THUD!

HA-HA! LUNCH! ALL TO THE DINING HALL!

COME ON, DOBBIN!

In the Dining Hall...

I'M NOW QUITE GLAD YOU BROUGHT DOBBIN ALONG!

OH, WHY, SIR?

PONK!

BECAUSE WE CAN BORROW DOBBIN'S NOSE BAG FOR FATTY! HA-HA-HA!

CHORTLE! YES! SAVED US BEING SPRAYED BY FOOD AS HE EATS!

CHOMP! MUNCH! GOBBLE!

CHOMP!

DOBBIN

CUT!

PUP PARADE

LATER — Thank goodness that rain's stopped — now we can get out...

One of us can't...

...Tubby's sunk in the mud!

Great, fat lump — I've an idea to get him out though.

Oooh, sausages — my very, very favourites!

Here, Tubby.

GLOOP!

He's free!

Erk!

SPLAT!

Any bright ideas on how to get the rest of the Pups out of the mud now, Bones?

Ahem!

IS IT TRUE OLD TRAFFORD'S DISAPPEARED?

NO, IT'S JUST A GROUNDLESS RUMOUR.

WE'RE AT AN 'OUTWARD BOUND' CAMP THIS WEEK. KIDS HAVE TO DO 'TASKS' AND IT MAKES THEM THINK! I HOPE! HEH-HEH!

OUTWARD BOUND CAMP

HERE'S YOUR FIRST TASK, TEACHER. GET THE KIDS OUT OF BED — IT'S 7 A.M.!

OKAY!

... ANYONE FOR OLIVE'S PRUNE, KIPPER AND CUSTARD PORRIDGE?

HORRIBLE NIFFS

Seconds later.

HA-HA! IT WORKED!

AWFUL!

GAG!

PHEW!

Later.

THE TASK IS TO MA YOUR WAY OVER T POND. YOU MAY U THESE ROPES OR B OF WOOD!

CO

OUTWARD BOUND

GET YOUR FLASK OF TEA OUT, TEACHER. THEY'LL BE HOURS IN THAT DARK WOOD!

OUTWA

Very soon —

YAHOO! MADE IT!

WOW! IN RECORD TIME!

FAILED!

OUTWA

WHAT FURNITURE IS MADE WITH STRIPPED PINE?

A WELSH UN-DRESSER.

dorm.

AKEY! WAKEY! RISE AND SHINE!

SNORT! GRUNT!

SNORE! WHEEZE!

SIGH! THEY DO THAT IN CLASS TOO!

SNORE!

THIS'LL WAKEN THEM! HAR-HAR!

SWOOSH

SWOOSH

HO-HO! NO! TOO WELL PROTECTED!

GRRR! I DIDN'T WANT TO HAVE TO DO THIS BUT . . .

ZZZZ!

'LL MAKE THINK!

Very soon.

FINISHED! WE DIDN'T EVEN HAVE TO USE THE ROPES AND WOOD!

EH?

WE 'MADE' STEPPING STONES!

SPLOSH!

SPLISH!

OW! OW!

GRRR! FAILED THIS TASK!

OO . . . ER!

Next —

YOUR NEXT TASK IS TO GO INTO THE CENTRE OF THIS VERY THICK WOOD AND MAKE YOUR WAY OUT AGAIN!

! CHEATS! DROPPED S ON THE WAY TO THE RE OF THE WOOD — N LET FATTY SNIFF THE CHOCOLATE TO GET BACK OUT!

URP! GREAT PLAN! DO IT AGAIN!

Later —

WELL, KIDS OF BASH STREET SCHOOL — YOU'VE PASSED THE OUTWARD BOUND COURSE!

WAHEY!

WELL I NEVER!

OUTWARD BOUND SCHOOL

PASS

WANT TO KNOW WHY THEY PASSED?

YAHOO! PASSED!

IF YOU FAIL — FEEL FREE TO COME BACK NEXT WEEK AND TRY AGAIN

GASP! WE JUST COULDN'T FACE ANOTHER VISIT!

WHY DID THE OX HAVE A SORE THROAT?

IT WAS A PROPER YAK.

FITNESS FUNATICS

EH? A TRUANT OFFICER?

HMMM!

SIGH! ANOTHER SCHOOL DAY

HE'S WATCHING TEACHER — NOT US!

I'M THE 'SCHOOL TEACHER FITNESS INSPECTOR'. I HAVE TO CHECK AND SEE IF TEACHERS ARE FIT ENOUGH TO DO THEIR JOB!

HUMPH!

HE'S GOT NO CHANCE!

AHEM! I AM A FAST MOVER!

WE'LL TEST YOU, SIR!

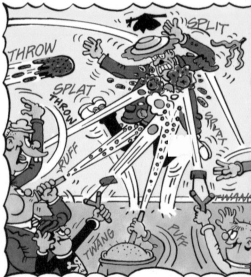

THROW

SPLIT

SPLAT

THROW

RUFF

TWANG

PUFF

TWANG

OKAY, KIDS. YOU'LL BE AWARDED A NEW, SUPER FIT TEACHER!

SNAP

FAIL

EH?

FIRST MATHS, THEN HISTORY FOLLOWED BY TWO HOURS OF ENGLISH!

AGH!

EH?

ZOOM

ZOOM

GASP!

NOT THAT!

NO, NEVER!

I KNOW HOW TO SAVE OUR TEACHER'S JOB!

Out in the playground.

SCHOOL CLOCK

WHAT MUSIC DO GIRL BANDS PLAY?

FROCK AND ROLL.

BE A SPORT

WHY DID THE BUTTERFLY GO TO THE BOOKIES?

IT FANCIED A FLUTTER!

LET ME READ IT!

I WANT TO HAVE A LOOK!

THIS IS TEACHER'S BOOK. WE'RE USING IT . . .

Reader's voice.

WOW! THEY'RE KEEN TO READ A BOOK! IT'S NEVER BEEN KNOWN BEFORE!

BRITISH BIRDS

ER . . . WE'LL LEAVE THE MATHS LESSON AND GO OUT FOR A . . . ER . . . NATURE LESSON! AHEM!

HEH-HEH! WE THOUGHT HE'D WANT TO DO THAT!

At the edge of the woods.

A REWARD FOR ANYONE WHO CAN POINT OUT THAT RARE BIRD!

CHORTLE!

TWEET! TWEET! HERE, TWEETER! TWEET!

HUH! HOW CAN WE FIND IT? WE'LL HAVE TO GET TEACHER OUT OF THE WAY SO THAT WE CAN ESCAPE FOR THE DAY!

YES!

SIR! SIR! UP THERE! IT'S UP THERE!

GOOD BOY!

TRYING TO SNEAK AWAY, WERE YOU?

WHEEEEEE

AAGH!

OOF!

CRASH

WE'D BETTER STICK TOGETHER!

HUH! WE'LL NEVER GET RID OF TEACHER NOW!

DAZED

HMM! I WOULDN'T SAY THAT! I'VE SPOTTED SOMETHING ELSE OF INTEREST!

LOOK SIR! I'VE SPOTTED THE HEADMASTER PLAYING GOLF!

SO IT IS! HE TELEPHONED THE SCHOOL TO SAY HE WAS ILL TODAY!

CHIP!

BOUNCE

...TO MAKE OUR OWN LESSER SPOTTED TWEETER BIRD! HA-HA!

WE'RE MAKING ONE OF THESE BIRDS!

RARE LESSER SPOTTED BIRD

PUSH

Later.

DRONE! BLAH! BORE!

THROW

SIR! SIR! WHAT KIND OF BIRD IS THAT?

BIRD? BIRD?

WOW! IT LOOKS LIKE A VERY RARE LESSER SPOTTED TWEETER BIRD!

HOP HOP

TITTER! DOES IT, SIR?

YOU'D BETTER CLIMB UP AND TAKE A CLOSE LOOK!

GOOD IDEA!

PUSH

TUM... TEE... TUM!

HEH-HEH! ONCE HE'S UP A BIT — WE'LL RUN FOR IT! CHORTLE!

ER... NO SIGN OF IT, PUPILS!

CREAK

CREAK

WAAAA!

SNAP

WHEEEEEE

HEADMASTER!

OO...ER...AHEM!

CRUMP!

WHISH

THWACK

RICHEEEEE

HA-HA! TO KEEP US QUIET THE HEAD'S GIVEN US THE REST OF THE DAY OFF!

AND TEACHER'S FORCED THE HEAD...

...INTO HELPING HIM LOOK FOR THE 'LESSER SPOTTED TWEETER'! CHORTLE!

FASTER, HEADMASTER! OR ELSE I'LL TELL ABOUT YOUR 'UNWELL SPELL' TODAY!

GASP! WHEEZE! OKAY!

HA-HA!

HO-HO!

TAKE THESE . . .

. . . TO MAKE SURE TO USE UP YOUR PENCILS TO THE VERY END!

HI!

YIKES!

PLOP

HMM!

YOU HAVE TO SHARE A SHEET OF PAPER WHEN WRITING!

FLIP

Then —

POP!

WAA!

EEK!

LOOK AT MY FEET!

SHIVER

GOOD!

ICE

YOU CAN SLIDE ON DOWN TO THE HEAD'S OFFICE TO COMPLAIN!

NO . . . STOP . . . UNHAND ME, PUPILS!

PUSH

SLIDE!

HEAD'S STUDY

WAA!

PUSH

SLIDE

HEH! HEH!

Soon —

PHEW! IT'S GETTING WARMER IN HERE!

TUG

YES! GASP!

In the Pizza Place.

TWO PIECES PLUS THREE PIECES EQUALS . . .

CHOMP! A NICE SNACK, SIR!

YOU SEE, READERS, TEACHER WASN'T TOO PLEASED TO DISCOVER THAT OUR HEAD WASN'T QUITE CUTTING BACK THE SPENDING OF SCHOOL FUNDS ON HIMSELF! CHORTLE!

WAH! CHEEK!

FLIP!

CAVIAR

CHOMP

CAFE POSH

WHAT TEACHER SAW THROUGH THE KEYHOLE

WHAT GIVES A HORSE THE TROTS?

STIRRUP OF FIGS.

PLUG

SPOTTY↓

DANNY

'ERBERT

SIDNEY↓

TOOTS↓

FATTY

WILFRED

SMIFFY

A CLOTHES ENCOUNTER

I HAVE A GREAT IDEA HOW TO GET TODAY OFF SCHOOL. ALL WE HAVE TO DO TO CONFUSE TEACHER IS . . .

Soon —

COME AWAY INTO CLASS, KIDS! HURRY UP!

DOH! I'D BETTER GO AND REST! CARRY ON . . . ER . . . DO SOMETHING BY YOURSELVES, CLASS!

HA-HA! GREAT PLAN TO CONFUSE TEACHER!

CHANGING CLOTHES HAS REALLY PUZZLED HIM! CHORTLE!

WHAT IS GOING ON IN HERE?

PONK!

IIB

TEACHER! I MUST TELL YOU OF AN EVIL PLAN TO CONFUSE YOU! THEY'VE ALL CHANGED CLOTHES!

POP

WOW!

HMM! CHANGED OUTFITS, EH!

VERY SNEAKY PLAN!

QUIET! SIT DOWN!

EH? THE JANITOR?

IIB

WHY IS THE ASTRONAUT WALKING UP THE STAIRS?

WE HAVE LIFT OFF.

SIT DOWN, DANNY!

I AM, SIR!

EH? WHAT ...?

WHAT'S GOING ON, FATTY?

I DON'T KNOW WHAT YOU MEAN, SIR!

P ... ER ... DANNY! ER ... LUG ... NO ... OO ...

SPLOOSH!

BLAZ

TWEAK

HUH! I WOULDN'T TAKE PART IN THEIR SILLY, CHILDISH PRANK. THEY WON'T LET ME OUT OF THE CLASS BECAUSE I'LL TELL TEACHER!

HEH-HEH! BUT I HAVE A 'SNEAK TUNNEL' UNDER MY DESK!

IT LEADS STRAIGHT TO THE STAFF ROOM! NNNGH!

O — I'M ...ACHER!

Then —

EVERYTHING OKAY, TEACHER?

HEH-HEH! YES!

Later —

ONE GOOD THING HAS COME OUT OF THIS DRESSING TO CONFUSE TRICK ...

BUT ... ER ...

... THE JANITOR IS OUR NEW 'OLIVE' AND HIS COOKING IS A THOUSAND TIMES BETTER THAN THE REAL OLIVE'S!

GRR! CHEEK! I'VE A GOOD MIND TO SACK YOU! I AM THE HEAD AFTER ALL!

MORE STEW, PLEASE!

CHOMP! CHORTLE!

ACTING THE FOOL!

One morning.

OOPS! SORRY, MISS!

WRONG ROOM!

IT'S NOT THE WRONG ROOM! SIT DOWN!

WHAT AN OUTFIT!

FANCY DRESS, SIR?

'TIS I! TARA!

HUMPH! SHOW OFF!

CHORTLE! THE BIG ENTRANCE! HEH-HEH!

START ACTING! NO SCRIPT — JUST IMPROVISE! ON WITH THE WORKSHOP!

TUG

GRR

WHEN HIS 9.30 SNACK'S FINISHED!

SOB! SUCH EMOTIONS OVER A SANDWICH!

BOO-HOO!

11.00 10.00
10.30
9.30 EMPTY

HO-HO! FATTY HAS TO WAIT TILL TEN O'CLOCK TO EAT AGAIN!

SNIFF! WONDERFUL ACTORS! WHERE DID YOU LEARN IT ALL? SNIFF!

PARP!

NATURAL TALENT, MISS!

AHA! I SEE! YOUR TEACHER HAS TAUGHT YOU ALL HE KNOWS!

EH?

DEFLATED

THE SCHOOL DRAMA TEACHER'S VISITING TODAY TO LEAD AN ACTING WORKSHOP! I'M JUST GETTING INTO THE ACTING MOOD!

STIFLED LAUGHTER

Then —

PROD
HONK

LINES

HARK! I HEAR THE SOUND OF TENDER FOOTSTEPS APPROACHING!

LINES

NICE BIT OF FREE-STYLE ACTING HERE, TEACHER!

BIFF
THUMP

OOF!

TAKE THAT!

OW!

CHORTLE! IT'S MORE LIKE FREE-STYLE WRESTLING, MISS!

Next —

GOSH! WOW! A POWERFUL PERFORMANCE! A VERY MOVING PIECE!

WAA! SOB! HOWL!

HUMP

HOWL! SOB! A WONDERFUL ACTOR!

HA-HA! WE SEE THIS EVERY DAY!

LOOK AT THAT ACTING! ...TERROR... INTER- ...NG WITH THE SITUATION!

SNARL! MY BEST WIG AND PAIR OF CURTAINS!

OO... ER!

NERVOUS ← CHEWING

CLUMP

HA-HA! IT'S REAL FEAR! THAT'S MRS TEACHER!

LOOK! MRS TEACHER'S FRYING PAN'S INTERACTING WITH TEACHER'S HEAD!

OW! OW!

TUG!

THUD

CLANG!

CHORTLE!

WHAT CROAKS WHEN YOU WALK?

A PAIR OF OPEN-TOAD SANDALS.

TEETHING TROUBLES

Early one morning.

NOW'S OUR CHANCE!

SNORE!

DOUGHNUTS ARE IMPOSSIBLE TO RESIST!

'GRAB'

HISHTORY FIRSHT, PUPILSH!

'SPRAY' THAT AGAIN, TEACHER! WE CAN'T UNDERSTAND YOU!

BLOOF!

SHTOP THISH NONSHENSH!

EH?

HEAD! HEAD! TEACHER'S SPITTING AT US!

I'M FURIOUSH — FURIOUSH!

I LIKE A NICE SHOWER!

HEH-HEH!

FALL

SCRUB

SCRUB

SHOWER GEL

HAW-HAW-HAW! WHAT A SCHEME!

TOPPLE

BUMP

YOWL!

LEAP

MAYBE I SHOULD HAVE PUT THESE MY BACK POCKE

TH

OO...E

HOW DO YOU START THE LOUDEST COCKEREL COMPETITION?

READY, STEADY, CROW!

EH-HEH!

I KNEW THEY'D BITE! TEACHER WON'T BE ABLE TO TEACH US WITHOUT TEETH!

So later.

WAIT FOR IT!

MUST DO SOMETHING ABOUT THIS!

Then —

WHAT'S GOING ON?

SHEASH THISH SHILLYNESH!

MY BEGONIA NEEDED WATERING. THANKS, TEACHER!

PYOING

Next —

SWISH

SHOWER GEL

SHO!

TAKE THISH NOTE TO YOUR PARENTSH!

TO BE DISINFECTED

...YOU SHTUPID, SHENSHLESH, WORSHLESH...

SPRAY

TO DANNY'S PARENTS

PAH!

CHUCKLE! I DON'T THINK MY PARENTS WILL MAKE MUCH SENSE OF THIS, NOW THAT TEACHER'S SPLATTERED IT!

PLASTIC SOLVENT

NOW TO DISHINFECT MY TEESH!

THAT'S WHAT HE THINKS!

WHAT IS THE WAR CRY OF A SMALL JAPANESE TREE?

BONSAI!

FUNNY NATURE

CLASS IIB

TODAY WE SHALL GO OUTSIDE TO STUDY NATURE!

OH, NO!

GRAB!

GLUE

I'LL NEED THIS!

WHERE IS THAT SILLY BOY, SMIFF?

HMM!

TWIRL!

WHEE!

COME ON, PULL ME SOUTH WITH YOU. I FANCY A SUNTAN!

But —

ZOO

TH

TUG!

ER . . . I'D BETTER LET HIM GO — HE'S NOT QUITE STRONG ENOUGH!

Next —

SOME ANIMALS PUT ON THICK WINTER COATS TO SURVIVE THE COLD WEATHER!

AW! THAT CHAP DOESN'T HAVE A WINTER COAT!

HOI!

HOW WOULD A SPANISH DANCER CATCH FISH?

CASTANET!

PROBLEM KIDS

OOH!

AAH!

HUM!

OOOOO!

Reader's voice.

OH, NO! THEY LOOK A[...] THEY'RE IN GREAT PA[...]

EEAAARGH!

ONE PUPIL PLUS ONE PUPIL EQUALS . . .

SIR! SIR! I'VE GOT THE ANSWER, SIR!

YES . . . YES . . .

ONE PUPIL PLUS ONE PUPIL EQUALS — A FIGHT! HA-HA-HA!

I'VE GOT A BETTER CARD THAN YOU!

YOU DON'T!

KICK

TWIST

Later.

THIS IS CHARLIE!

PUZZLED!

CLASS IIB

UGH! UGH!

IF CHARLIE GETS THE CORRECT ANSWER TO A PROBLEM . . .

5-3

OOGH! OOGH!

. . .HE'S GIVEN A PEANUT AS A REWARD!

LIFT

PLOP

HMM! LET'S TRY IT ON THE KIDS!

OT QUITE! I'VE SET THEM A HEMATICAL PROBLEM AND HEY'RE FINDING IT TOO DIFFICULT!

ER... CAN WE HAVE A CLUE, SIR?

GASP!

IS IT A TRICK QUESTION?

I WILL NOT BE BEATEN! I'LL DEMONSTRATE THIS PROBLEM!

THIS WAY!

EH?

TUG

LIFT

Outside class IIB.

WE ARE DELIGHTED TO HAVE YOU HERE FROM THE INSTITUTE OF NEW TEACHING METHODS, PROFESSOR VON BRAIN!

CHOMP! OOH! I CAN'T TEACH THEM ANYTHING!

AHEM!

HMM! VERY INTERESTING!

YOU ARE IN NEED OF THE 'CHARLIE' METHOD OF TEACHING HERE! WAIT A MINUTE!

CLASS IIB

BEGIN, CLASS!

SLURP! SLOO!

2+2 =
5+1 =
1+2 =

ONE PLUS TWO EQUALS... THREE!

SUPER!

LIFT

SPIN

Later —

NNNGH! THE METHOD WORKS BUT NOW THERE'S A PROBLEM OF GETTING THE NEW 'SMARTER' KIDS OUT OF THEIR DESKS! HEAVE!

STRAIN

STUCK

HO-HO! YOU CAN'T WIN, TEACHER!

HO-HO! THE KIDS HAVE ANSWERED SO MANY QUESTIONS CORRECTLY — THEY'VE PUT ON LOTS OF WEIGHT!

UGH! UGH!

PUP PARADE